READ IT!!

(NO MORE EXCUSES)

Cover Design by Michael Males
Cover Photography by Jessica Ballew
Book Layout Concept Design by Rod Goelz
Music Edited by Scott Anderson

The Fingerboard

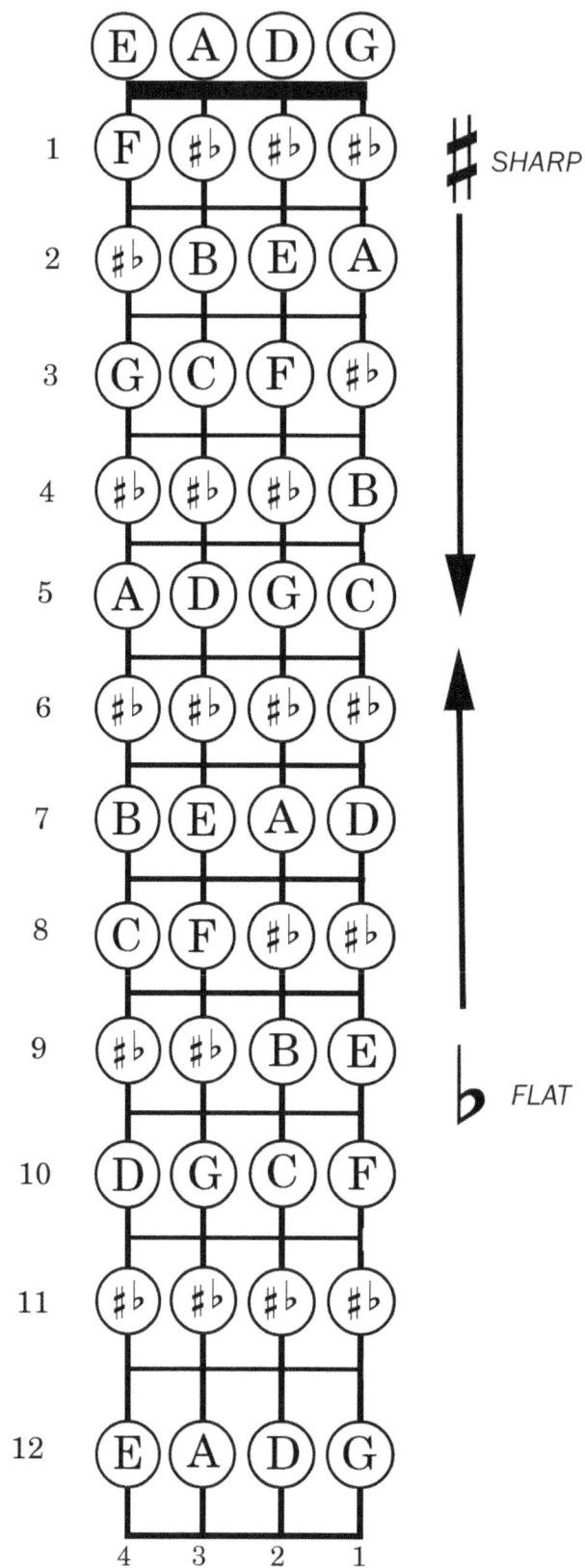

	4	3	2	1
	E	A	D	G
1	F	#♭	#♭	#♭
2	#♭	B	E	A
3	G	C	F	#♭
4	#♭	#♭	#♭	B
5	A	D	G	C
6	#♭	#♭	#♭	#♭
7	B	E	A	D
8	C	F	#♭	#♭
9	#♭	#♭	B	E
10	D	G	C	F
11	#♭	#♭	#♭	#♭
12	E	A	D	G

♯ SHARP

♭ FLAT

2

The Electric Bass

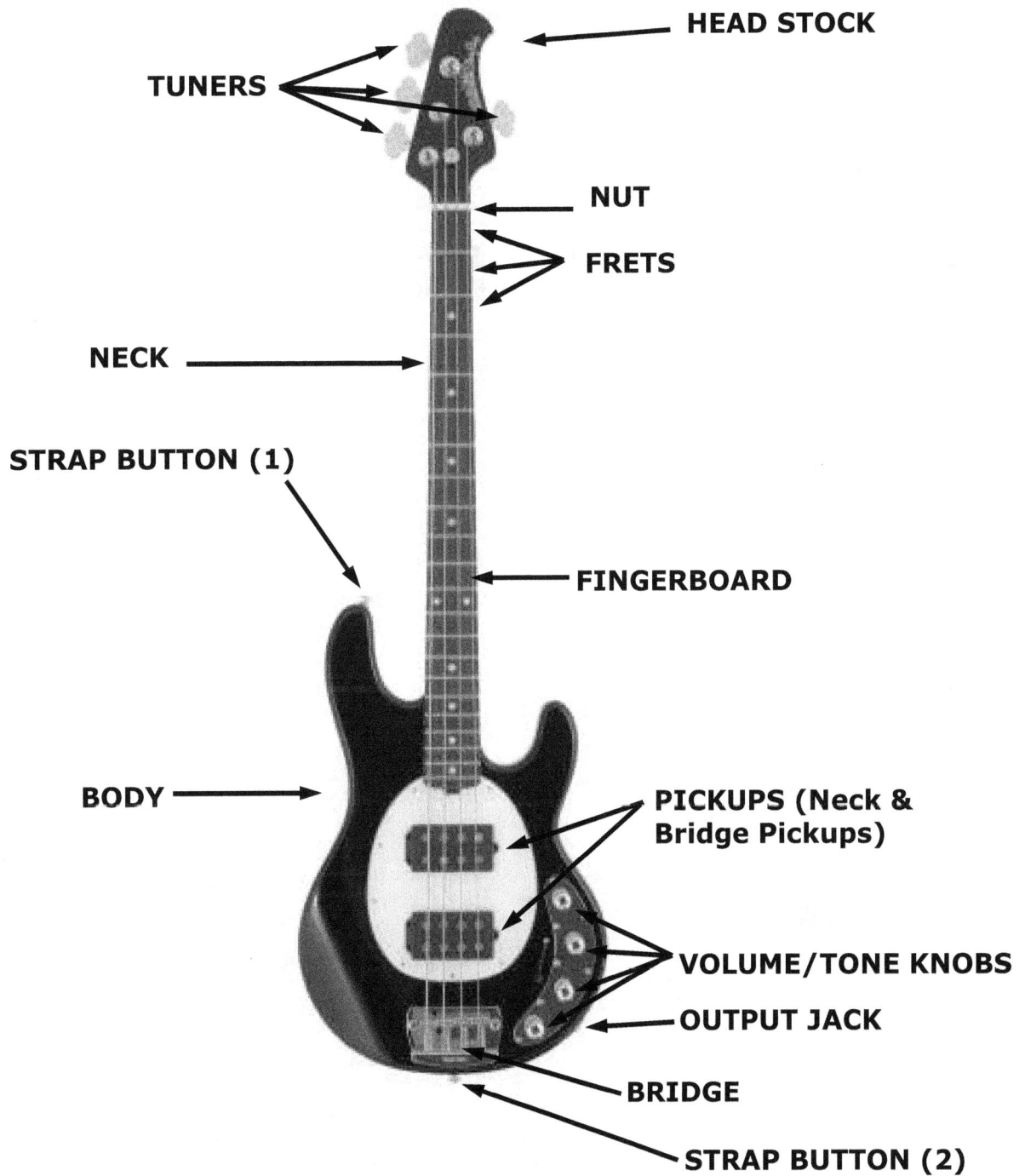

HEAD STOCK

TUNERS

NUT

FRETS

NECK

STRAP BUTTON (1)

FINGERBOARD

BODY

PICKUPS (Neck & Bridge Pickups)

VOLUME/TONE KNOBS

OUTPUT JACK

BRIDGE

STRAP BUTTON (2)

Musicman Stingray-Style Electric Bass

THE BASS CLEF

This is the BASS CLEF. Because of the range of our instrument, all music bass players read uses this clef. It's also referred to as the "F-Clef"—the line that goes between the two dots is the F line, and therefore the F note.

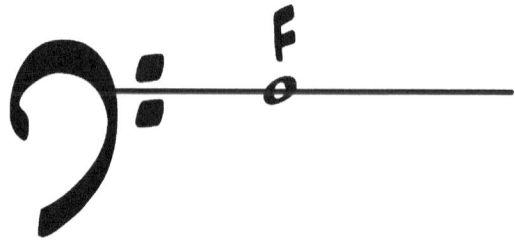

THE STAFF

THE LINES

Remember: **G**OOD **B**OYS **D**O **F**INE **A**LWAYS

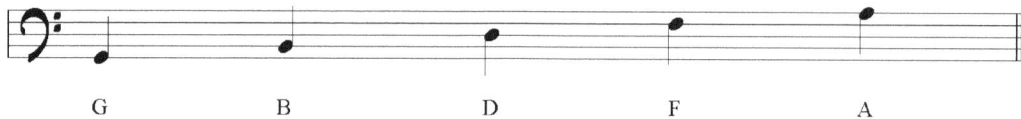

G   B   D   F   A

THE SPACES

Remember: **A**LL **C**OWS **E**AT **G**RASS

A   C   E   G

ABOVE AND BELOW (LEDGER LINES)

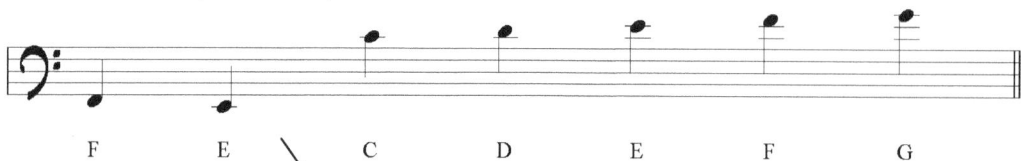

F   E   C   D   E   F   G

LEDGER LINES are used to extend the staff beyond the normal range of our instrument. Some notes are more commonly found than others (low E is far more common than high G).

4

READING TIME SIGNATURES

The *Time Signature* is THE essential tool for understanding the meter of a tune. It indicates how the notes are organized in two ways: 1) how many beats per measure;, and 2) what note fills up one beat. So much of what we all listen to is organized into groupings of four quarter notes pulses per measure. It's this pulse that we groove to, nod our head to, move to, dance to, and so much more within the musical experience.

4 FOUR BEATS PER MEASURE

4 THE TYPE OF NOTE RECEIVING THE BEAT (THE QUARTER NOTE)

C This symbol means COMMON TIME, another way of writing 4/4.

Meter within music can be organized in a variety of different ways. In this book, we'll examine two other commonly used time signatures.

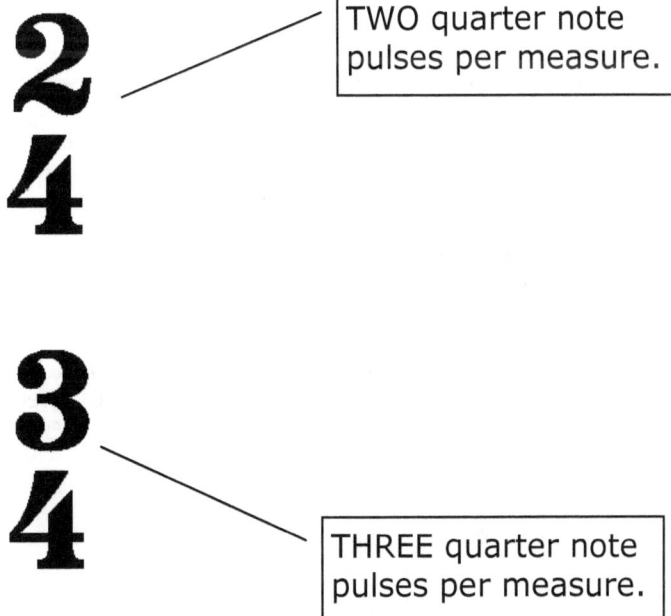

2
4 — TWO quarter note pulses per measure.

3
4 — THREE quarter note pulses per measure.

Basic Rhythms

The Whole Note (4 Counts)

Count: 1 (2   3   4)

The Half Note (2 Counts)

Count: 1   (2)   3   (4)

The Quarter Note (1 Count)

Count: 1   2   3   4

The Eighth Note (1/2 Count)

Count: 1 & 2 & 3 & 4 &

THE RESTS

To REST means to bring about SILENCE. Each rhythm above has a corresponding REST. They are: 1) The WHOLE Rest—4 beats of silence; 2) The HALF Rest—2 beats of silence; 3) The QUARTER Rest—1 Beat of silence; and 4) The EIGHTH Rest—1/2 beat of silence.

1.   2.   3.   4.

MUSICAL NAVIGATION

(Directional Signs)

REPEAT SIGNS

Repeat back to the "mirroring" repeat sign, or the beginning of the song if no "mirroring" repeat sign is provided.

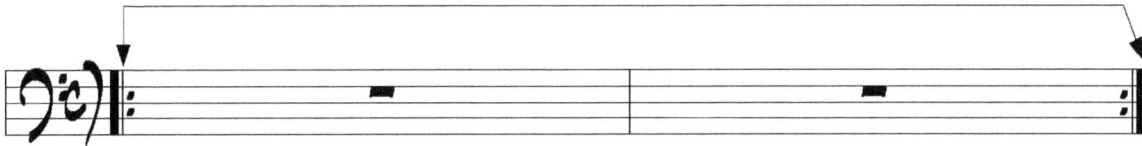

% ← Repeat the previous measure.

2
// ← Repeat the previous two measures.

ENDING SIGNS

First time through—TAKE THE FIRST ENDING. Repeat. Second time through, SKIP the first ending, TAKE THE SECOND ENDING.

1.

2.

D.S. AL CODA??

D.S. AL CODA

D.S. means go back to the Segno sign; proceed through the piece until you see the "to Coda" marking... jump to the Coda sign...finish out the tune!

𝄋 ← Segno Sign

𝄌 ← Coda Sign

READING SCALE DIAGRAMS

A scale is the consecutive arrangement of pitches from high to low and vice versa. One of the most common ways of displaying scales visually is through the use of scale diagrams. The example below shows the scale diagram as it as it appears in this book. Let's take a closer look.

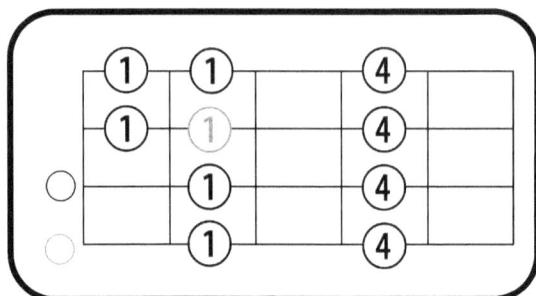

- The horizontal lines parallel the four strings of the bass— the top line represents the string closet to the floor; bottom line represents the string closest to your chin.

- The vertical lines resemble the fret bars.

- The numbered white circles are notes which make up the scale. The numbers represent the left-hand finger each note within the scale should be played with.

1=index; 2=middle; 3=ring; 4=pinky.

- The note in the lighter gray coloring indicates the ROOT NOTE of the scale.

To play through this pattern, start at the root tone and gradually ascend through the scale one scale degree at a time until you hit the highest note Descend one scale degree at a time to the note you started with— the root note! It's as simple as that!!

READING SCALE/MELODY NOTATION

FRETTING HAND FINGERING

STRING NUMBER

G = 1; D = 2; A = 3; E = 4

8

E STRING NOTES

4th String/OPEN

E

4th String/1st Fret/1st Finger

F

4th String/3rd Fret/3rd Finger

G

E STRING EXERCISES

①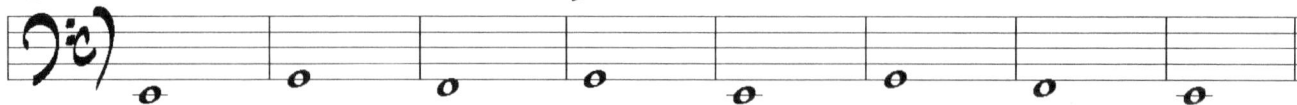

REVIEW: WHOLE NOTES = 4 COUNTS

②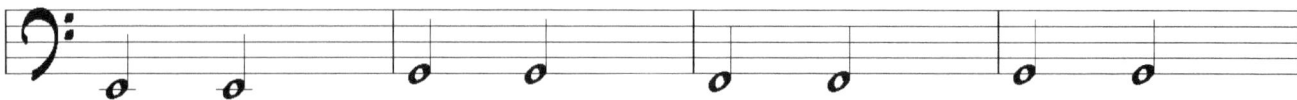

REVIEW: HALF NOTES = 2 COUNTS

③

REVIEW: QUARTER NOTES = 1 COUNT

④

⑤

⑥

A STRING NOTES

3rd String/OPEN

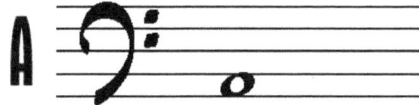

A

3rd String/2nd Fret/2ndFinger

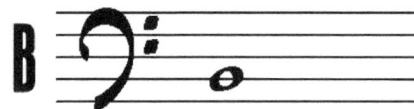

B

3rd String/3rd Fret/3rd Finger

C

A STRING EXERCISES

①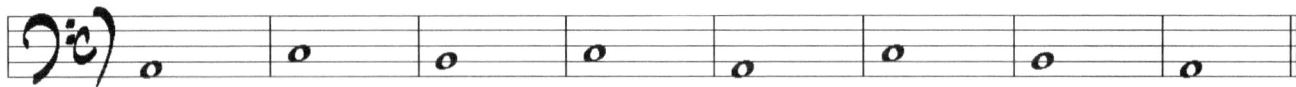

②

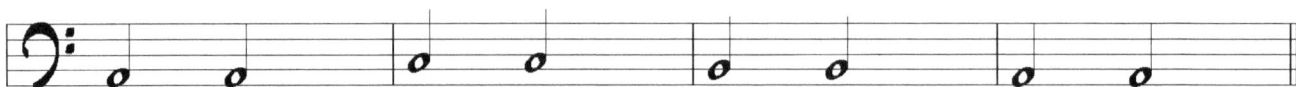

③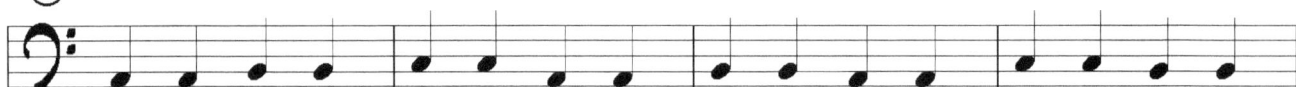

④

⑤

⑥

COMBINATION STUDIES 1

①

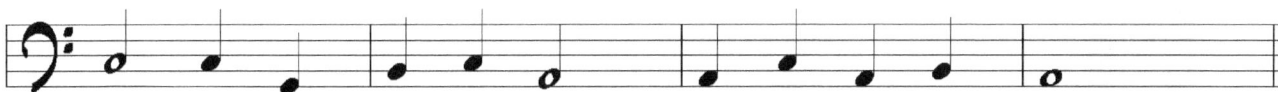

②

③

④

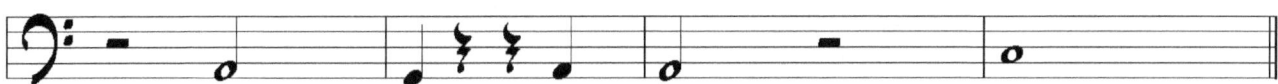

D STRING NOTES

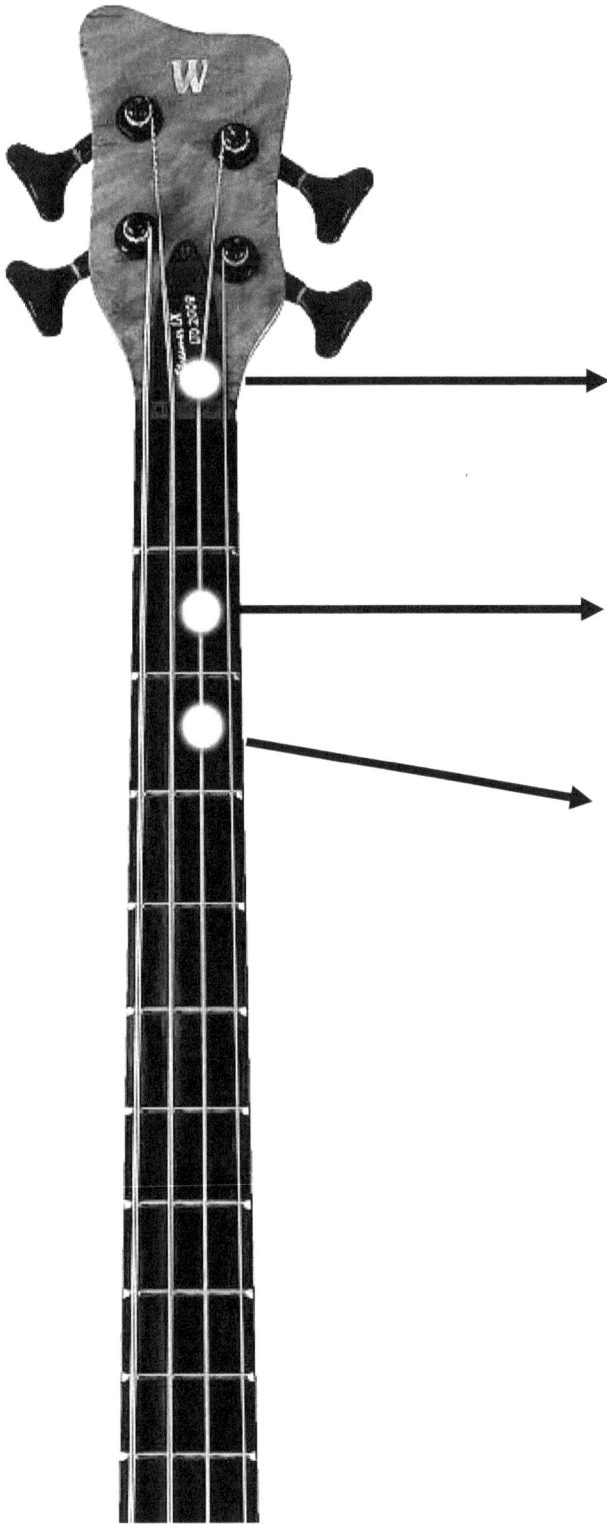

2nd String/OPEN

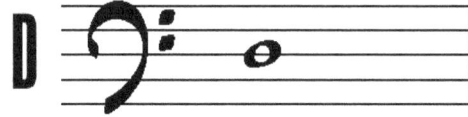

D

2nd String/2nd Fret/2ndFinger

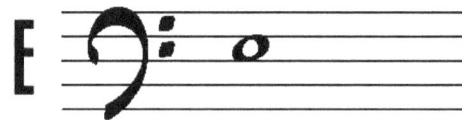

E

2nd String/3rd Fret/3rd Finger

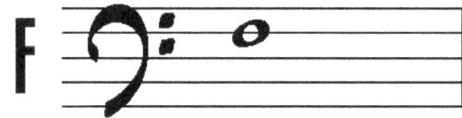

F

14

D STRING EXERCISES

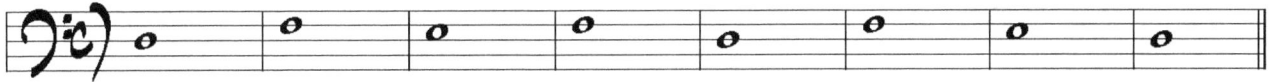

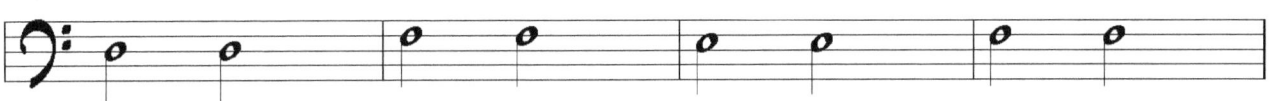

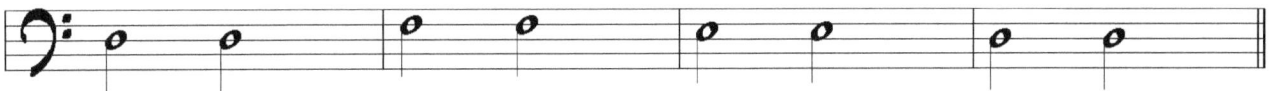

G STRING NOTES

1st String/OPEN

G

1st String/2nd Fret/1st Finger

A

1st String/4th Fret/3rd Finger

B

G STRING EXERCISES

COMBINATION STUDIES 2

BLUEGRASS 1

METAL 1A

METAL 1B

METAL 2A

METAL 2B

THREE FOUR TIME/DOTTED HALF NOTE

3 *beats per measure*

4 *4 = quarter note*

The Dot Rule

When you place a dot with a note, you increase the value of that by 1/2.

The dotted half note to the left is worth 3 beats (2+1=3)

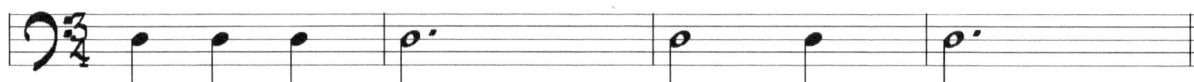

1970'S PIANO BALLAD STYLE

C   C/B   Ami   G

F   Emi   D   G

C   C/B   Ami   G

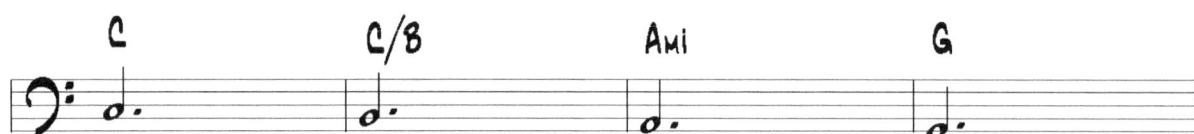

F   G   C   F/C

G/C   F/C   C   F/C

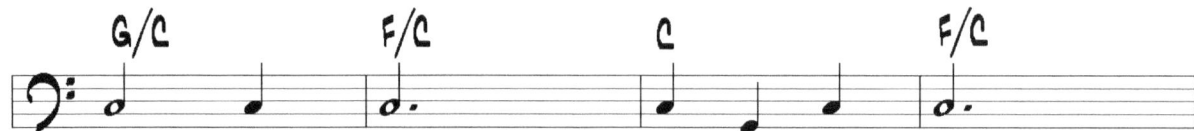

G/C   F/C   C

THREE ESSENTIAL ACCIDENTALS

THE SHARP SIGN *raises* the pitch (ABCDEFG) by one half step (1 fret).

b THE FLAT SIGN *lowers* the pitch (ABCDEFG) by one half step (1 fret)..

♮ The NATURAL SIGN *cancels out* a pre-existing SHARP or FLAT sign, returning the note to it's natural (ABCDEFG) state.

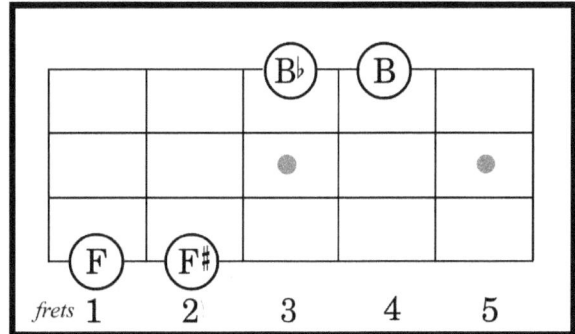

The *accidental's* power is short lived, it lives within the measure in which it was created. New measure = the note going back to natural (unaffected) state.

STRING NUMBER ④   ③   ②   ①

①   ②   ③   ④

VAN MORRISON STYLE

Ami7   Bmi7   Ami7   Bmi7   Ami7   Bmi7   Ami7   Bmi7

Ami7   Bmi7   Ami7   Bmi7   Ami7   Bmi7   Ami7   Bmi7

KEY SIGNATURES

This is a key signature.

Key Signatures indicate what notes are to be universally *sharped* or *flatted* throughout a song. Note that there is one sharp (F#) in the Key Signature. This indicates that all F notes (all octaves) need to raised a half step. So true with all Key Signatures.

"NO DOUBT" LOW END VARIATIONS

Var. 4

Var. 5

THE TIE

Think of the tie as a musical trailer hitch— attaching two notes together, thus creating one longer rhythm that is the sum of the two. Strike the first note, don't strike the second—hold on to that note until the next untied rhythm (beat two of the second measure in the example below).

BASIC RHYTHM STUDIES IN 4/4

10

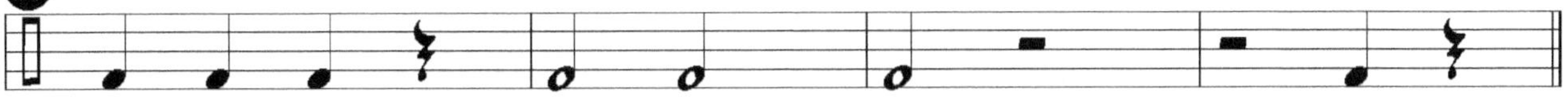

11

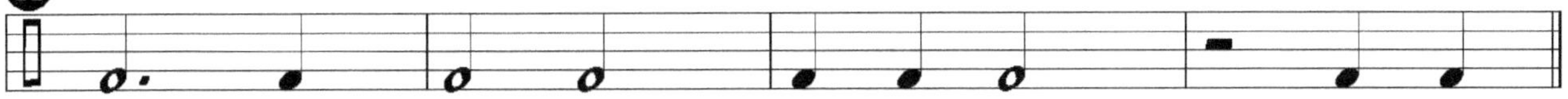

12

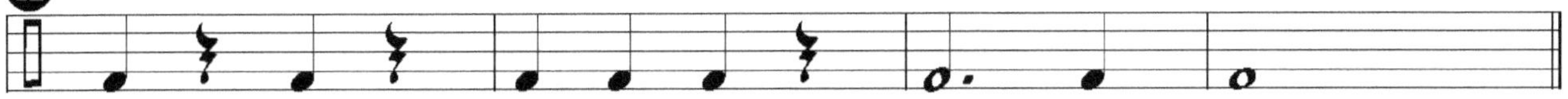

13

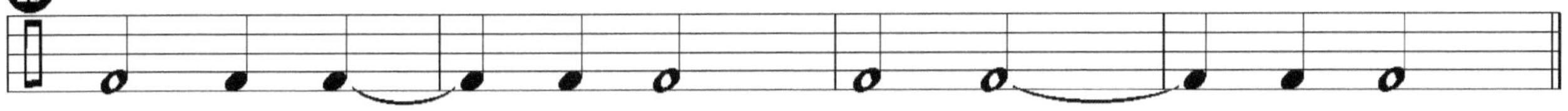

14

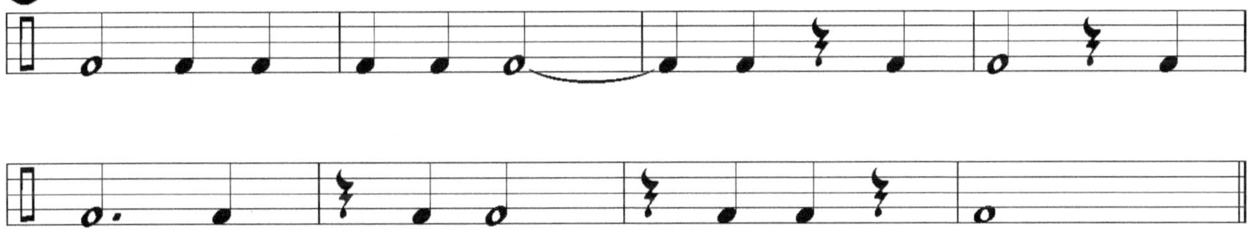

15

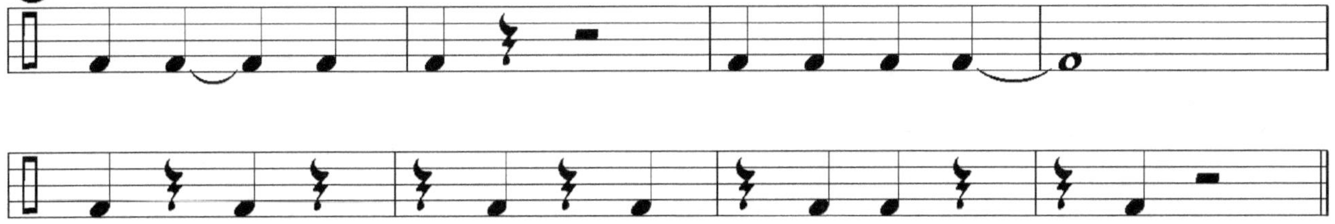

16

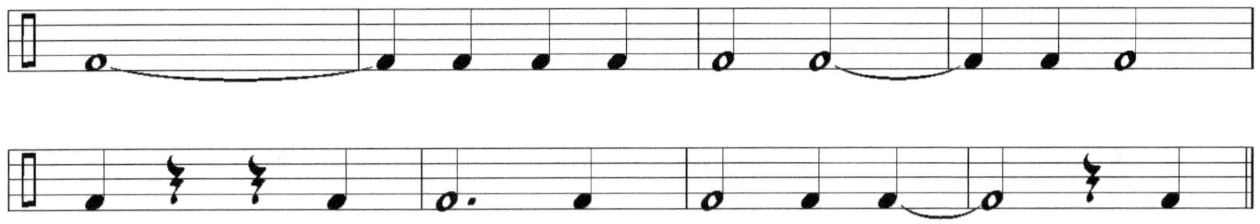

UP THE NECK (PART ONE)

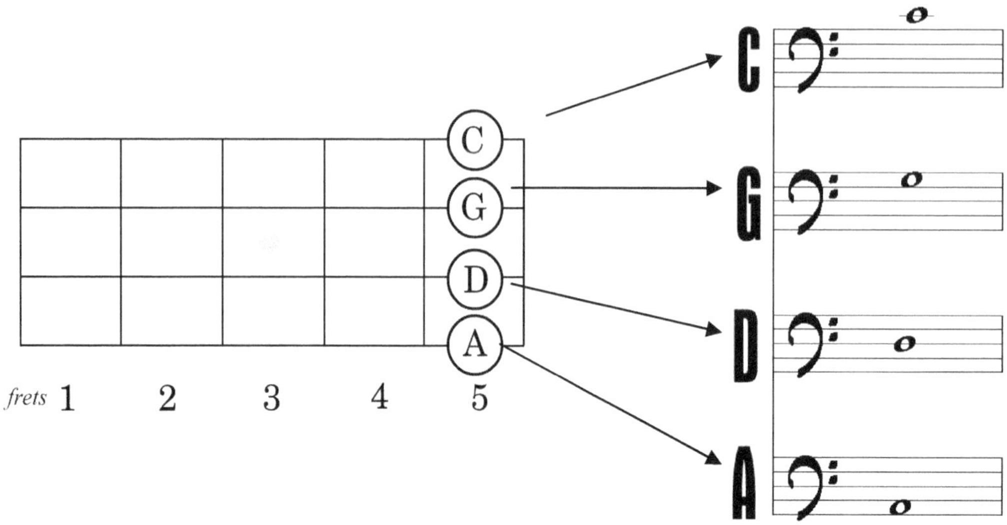

C Major (2nd Position)

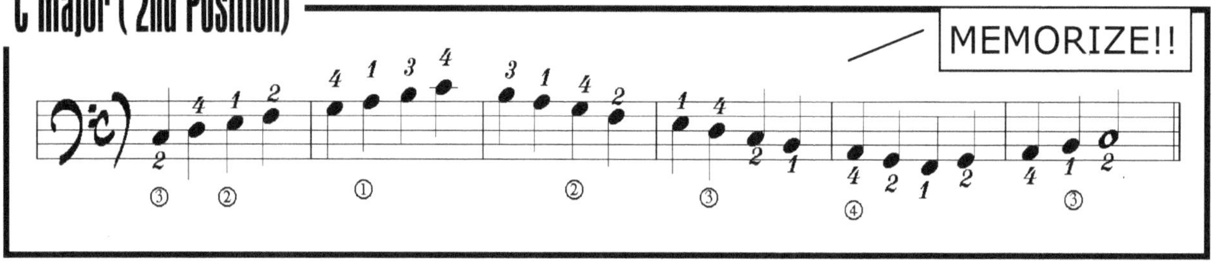

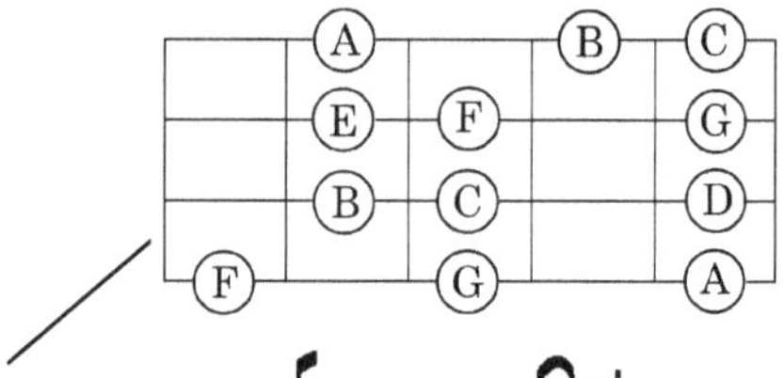

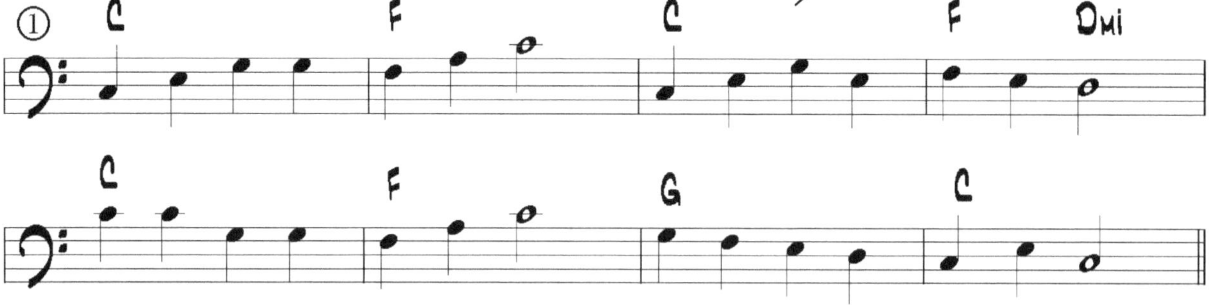

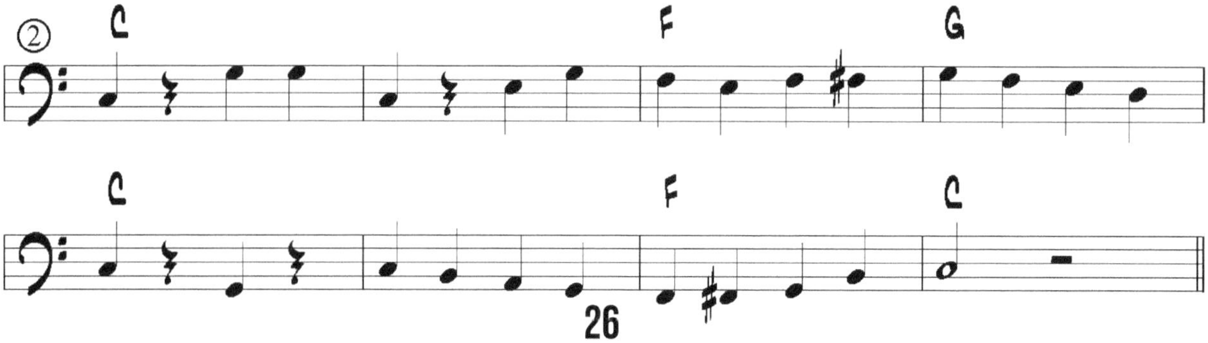

PAUL McCARTNEY STYLE 1

"The fat boy in the back was the bass player, and who wanted to be him? ... But then I started to see some interesting things in it. One of the very earliest was in 'Michelle.' There's that descending bass line thing... and I found that if I played a C, and then went to a G, and then to a C, it really turned the phrase around. It gave it a musicality that the descending chords just hadn't got. It was lovely. And it was one of my first sort of awakenings: 'Ooh, ooh, the bass really can change the track.'"

Paul McCartney/The Beatles

WHAT'S IN A SONG (SONG FORM)?

THE VERSE — A

- Characters--the cast of characters is introduced, their story unfolds...
- Narrative--the Verse supplies the details, history, and play-by-play facts that our story requires.
- The Verse is not repetitive (unlike the chorus). Each verse contains different words—MORE STORY LINE.

THE CHORUS — B

- The Chorus contains the "hook" of the song, the most memorable lyrical line within the song. The "hook" often generates the song's title.
- The Chorus is often repetitive, using the same or similar words from Chorus to Chorus.

THE TRANSITIONAL BRIDGE — T

- This bridge serves as a musical transition between the verse and chorus, supplying a smoother musical resolution than a Verse/Chorus can offer.
- Occurs multiple times throughout the course of a song.
- The Transitional Bridge is also known as the pre-chorus.

THE PRIMARY BRIDGE — C

- Attempts to make sense out of the story being told, often in a philosophical way.
- Completely new musical idea, new chords, melodies, etc.
- Occurs only once within a song, usually after the second chorus.

G Major (2nd Position)

MEMORIZE!!

> "I have to wonder why so many musicians with professional aspirations have resisted learning the **#1 academic skill** that could help them achieve their goal... **reading music."**

Jeff Berlin

MY CHEMICAL ROMANCE STYLE (EXPANDED)

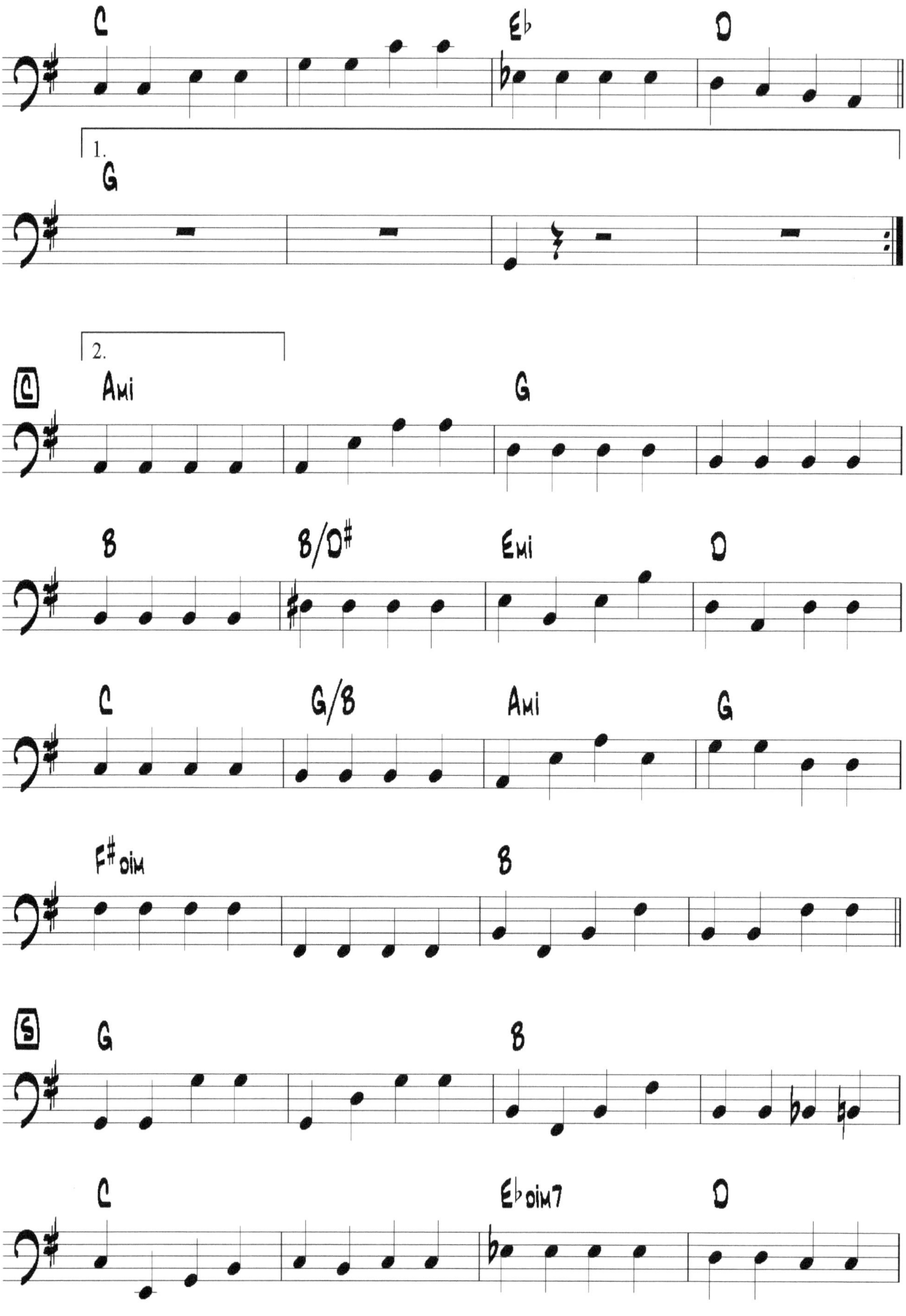
C
E♭
D
1.
G
2.
C
Ami
G
B
B/D#
Emi
D
C
G/B
Ami
G
F#dim
B
S
G
B
C
E♭dim7
D

G   B

C   E♭oiM7 D G

STANDUP BASS FINGERINGS 101

Upright bass scale fingerings, though different than traditional "guitar-based" fingerings, can be adapted to the electric bass with great success! "Guitar"-based fingering employ a "finger-per-fret" organizational mindset. On the "upright", the third finger is a support finger—used to support the fourth finger—an unused finger otherwise. With this in mind, upright fingerings when adapted to the electric bass avoid the third finger altogether (for there is no need for a support finger on the electric bass. These fingerings relieve stress on fretting hand by shifting the pinky in a fret. While this book focuses on "reading," you'll find these fingering to be useful in all areas of playing.

F MAJOR (UPRIGHT ADAPTATION)

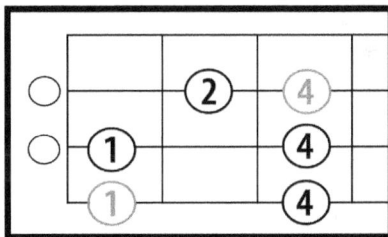

A MAJOR STUDIES (UPRIGHT FINGERING)

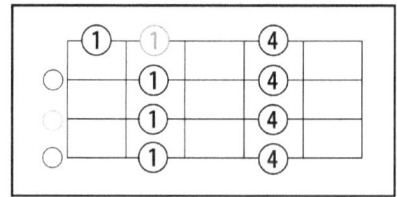

E MAJOR STUDIES (UPRIGHT FINGERING)

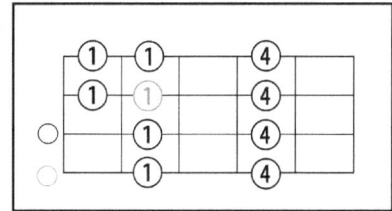

F MAJOR STUDIES (UPRIGHT FINGERING)

36

Bb MAJOR STUDIES (UPRIGHT FINGERING)

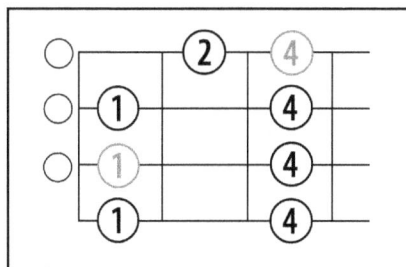

1940's SWING STYLE

ALBERT COLLINS/JOHNNY B. GAYDEN STYLE

CHUCK BERRY/WILLIE DIXON STYLE

SINGLE STRING READING: A STRING

note	A	B	C	D	E	F	G	A
fret	0	2	3	5	7	8	10	12

"SAY AS YOU PLAY" DUKE IN A

"The variety of musical literature is so vast, and the skills that can be obtained by learning some of this literature are so profound, that I view players who make a conscious decision not to read as very unfortunate. It's sad that so many players miss the chance to elevate their musicality by choosing not to learn how to read."

Jeff Berlin

"SAY AS YOU PLAY" PINK FLOYD

SINGLE STRING READING: E STRING

note	E	F	G	A	B	C	D	E
fret	0	1	3	5	7	8	10	12

"SAY AS YOU PLAY" DUKE IN E

"*The best way to learn to read is to be in a situation where you're forced to read. In high school I memorized one of the stage-band parts and pretended to be reading, so people got the impression I was an incredible sight-reader. They started recommending me to sub for anybody, so I quickly had to get my reading together! A key to sight-reading is to try to read a bar ahead. You should also scan the chart when you first get it to find the most difficult part, so you can figure it out before you have to perform it.*"

Nathan East/L.A. Studio

41

SINGLE STRING READING: D STRING

note	D	E	F	G	A	B	C	D
fret	0	2	3	5	7	9	10	12

"SAY AS YOU PLAY" DUKE IN D

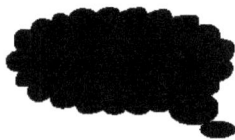

> "Tablature doesn't give what is actually there, it just shows you where to place your hands. If a person learns how to do that, if they can learn where the notes are on the neck, then they can learn how to read. It is easy to learn how to read... I don't understand when people go to tab. As a matter of fact every time I do something and someone asks me for a bass line in Tab, I flat out say, 'I don't understand it and I don't do Tab.'"

Chuck Rainey

42

SINGLE STRING READING: G STRING

note	G	A	B	C	D	E	F	G
fret	0	2	4	5	7	9	10	12

"SAY AS YOU PLAY" DUKE IN G

READING SCALE/MELODY NOTATION (PART 2)

You may have noticed that the Scale & Melody Notation that was so important in the first part of the book is easing up a bit. This is intentional. As your reading skills improve, your need for the Melody Notation decreases. In the pages that follow, I will be using these tools less and less, by giving some of the information (1 string number), while letting you make fingering, scale, and position decisions on your own. It's part of the process!

43

THE EIGHTH NOTE

The EIGHTH NOTE is an easy rhythm. Take the QUARTER NOTE rhythm... divide it into two equal parts... PRESTO... you have yourself an eighth note.

"BETTER THAN EZRA" STYLE

U2/ADAM CLAYTON STYLE

NICKELBACK 1

NICKELBACK 2

NICKELBACK 3

OLD TIME GROOVE ONE

OLD TIME GROOVE TWO

45

OLD TIME GROOVE THREE

SLY STONE/VICTOR WOOTEN STYLE

OLD TIME GROOVE FOUR

"I just don't understand why they don't sit down and learn where 'G' is on the neck."

Chuck Rainey

47

UP THE NECK (PART TWO)

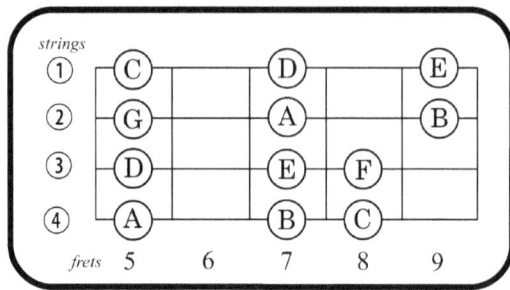

A NATURAL MINOR SCALE
(5th Position)

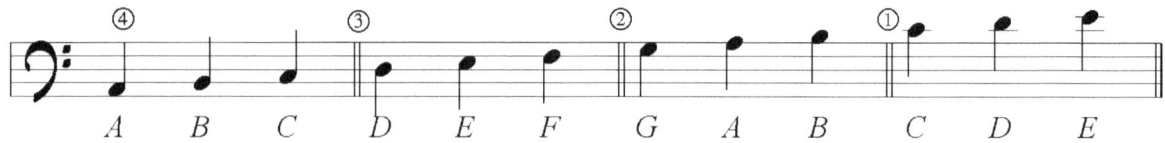

A B C D E F G A B C D E

"SAY AS YOU PLAY" (5th POSITION)

Directions: SAY the notes as you PLAY the notes. All notes and fingerings are in fifth position

"SAY AS YOU PLAY" (5th POSITION)

Directions: SAY the notes as you PLAY the notes. All notes and fingerings are in fifth position (frets 5-9).

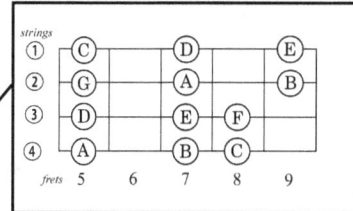

OLD TIME GROOVE FOUR (in A)

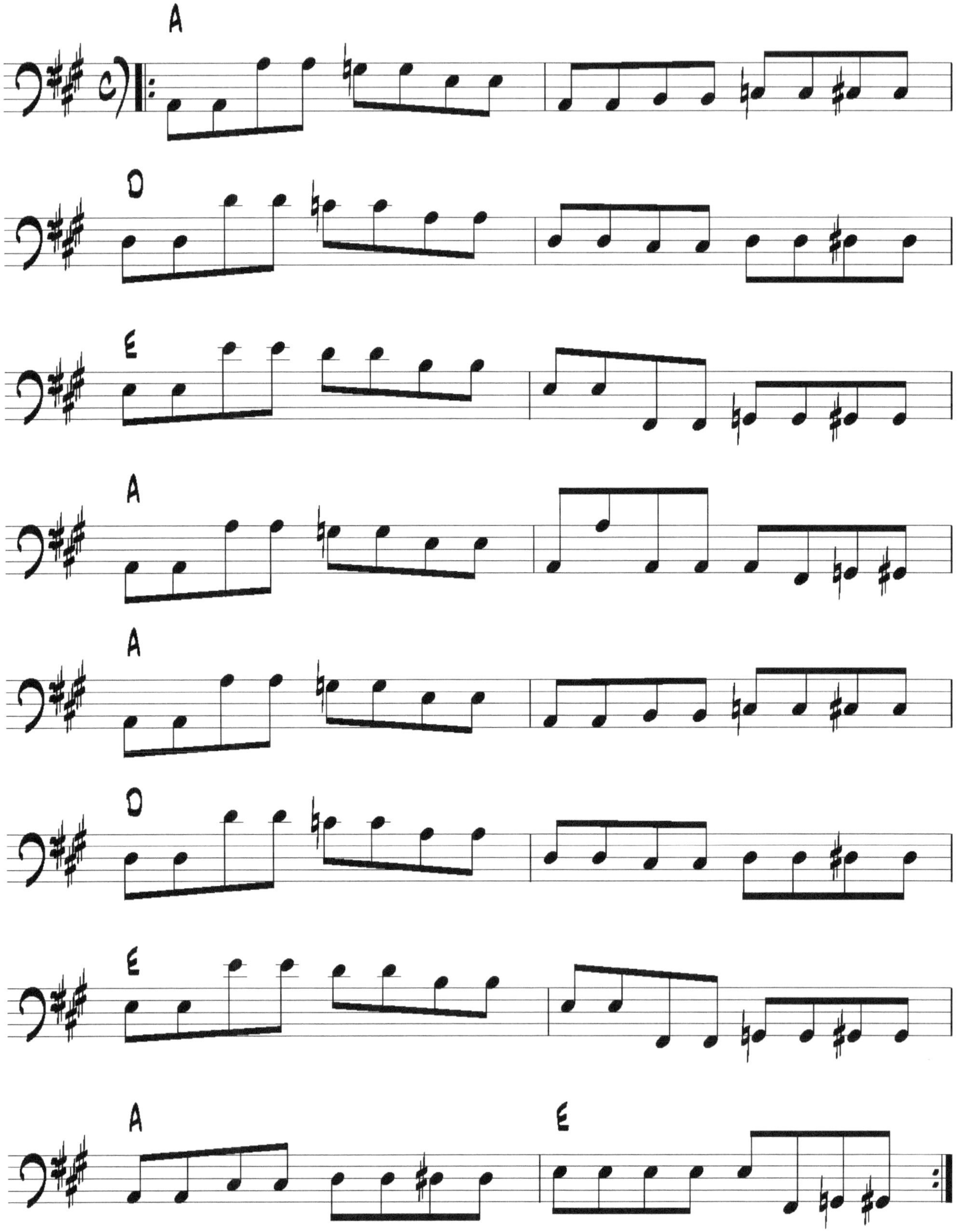

MICHAEL JACKSON: "SAY AS YOU PLAY"

SHARPED notes can be pronounced with one syllable: eese.

For example: FEESE (F#), CEESE (C#), GEESE (G#), etc.

KURT COBAIN: "SAY AS YOU PLAY"

8th NOTE RHYTHM STUDIES (PART 1)

10

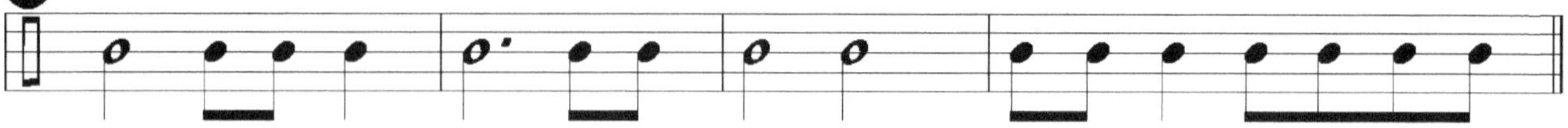

11

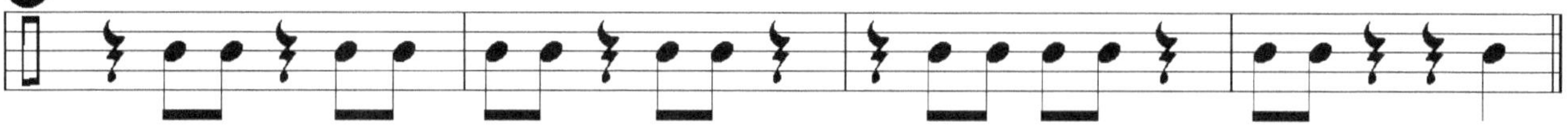

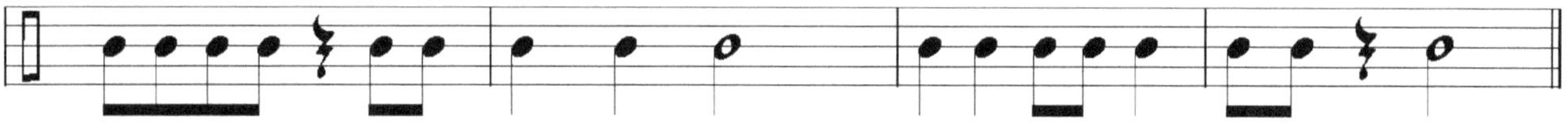

13

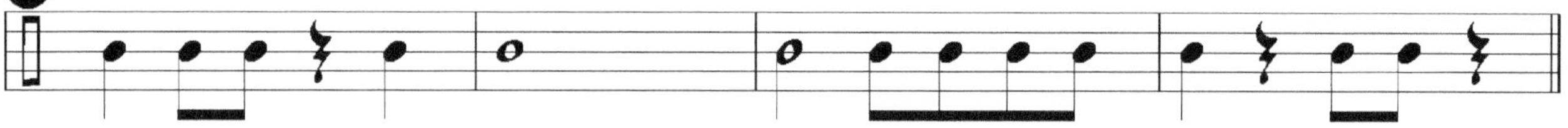

14

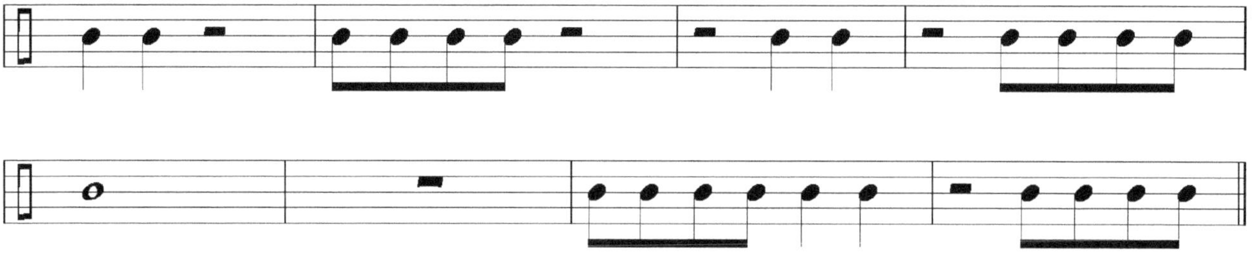

15

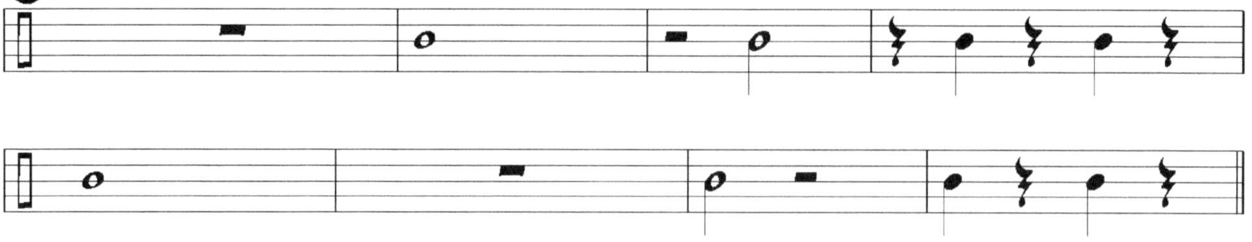

16

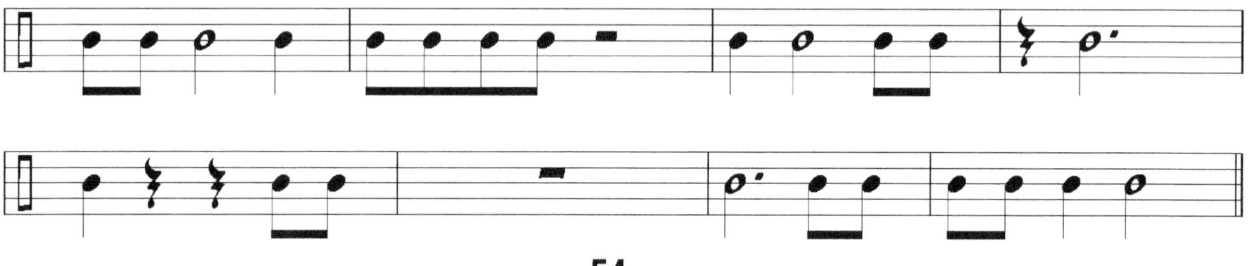

DOTTED QUARTER/8th COMBINATION

NEW RHYTHM?

1½ beats in duration; almost always coupled with the single 8th note (shown below). COUNT: **ONE** two **AND THREE** four.

17

18

19

20

21

NEW RHYTHM?

22

23

24

25

26

8th/QUARTER/8th COMBINATION:

COUNT: **ONE AND** two **AND** **THREE** four.

NEW RHYTHM?

27

28

29

30

31

57

CLASSIC 8th NOTE ROCK RIFFS

CLASSIC 8th R&B RIFFS

10

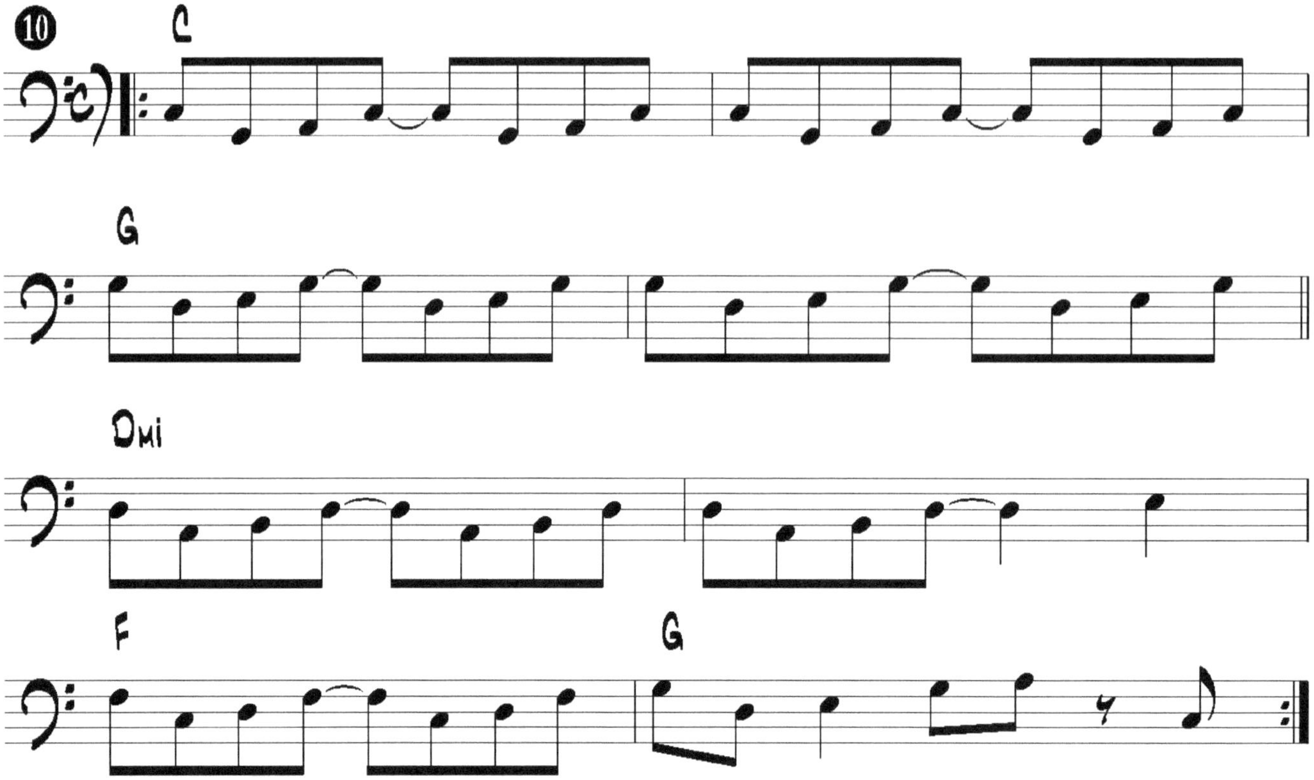

11

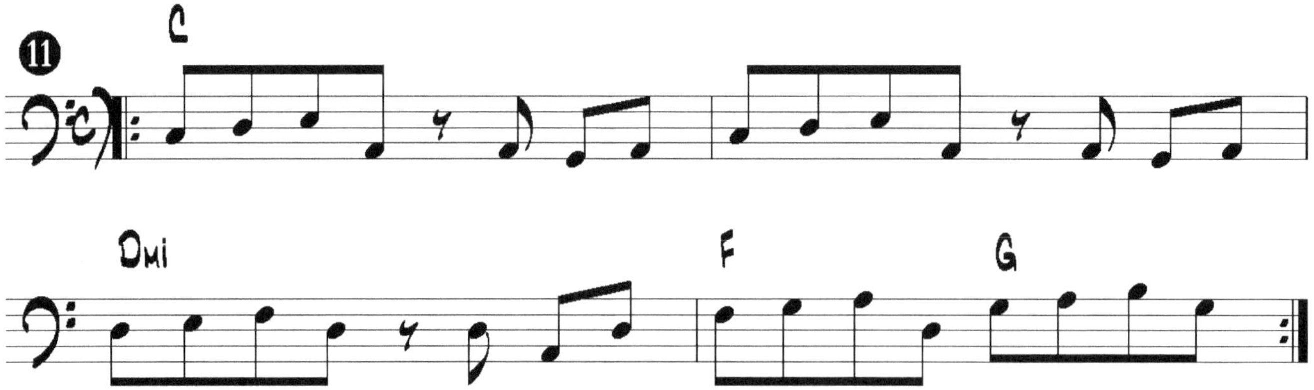

12

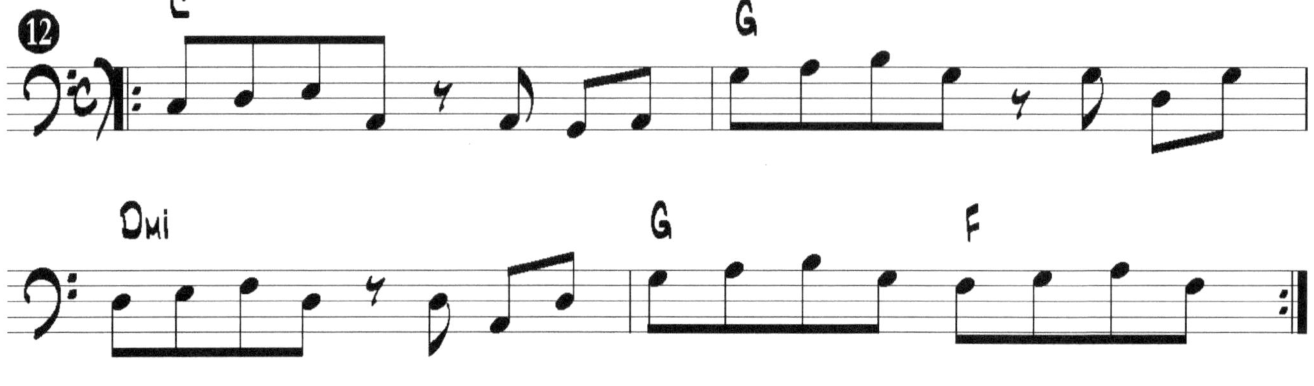

"Take what you do very seriously, and work hard at it. It doesn't matter if you solo. You're the bass player, the bottom—you drive the band. When I was growing up, everyone said, "Oh, it's just a second guitar." B.S.! It's an art, man. Get a James Jamerson record. We should all be proud to be bass players."

Matt Freeman/Rancid

WILSON PICKETT/STAX STYLE

"The best advice I have for any young musician is to learn as much as you can and develop as many different things on your instrument as you can. Everyone's dream is to play exactly the music you want, the way you want. But you never know what will happen. You want to give yourself the best chance for success possible. You do this by being ready for any situation that comes along. At the same time though, never lose sight of your own dreams and never give up. And most of all practice every day."

Victor Bailey

DRIFTERS STYLE BAION

"I think things come and go but people are always gonna get excited about great musicians. I think it's important to use your cultural influences in your music, too. That's what's gonna set you apart from everybody else!"

Marcus Miller

PHIL SPECTOR BAION STYLE

"I'll read through drum books. That's a great idea for bass players--you use your right-hand fingers as drum sticks."

Jeff Andrews/Vital Information

BRIAN WILSON BAION STYLE

"Today the word 'technique' is usually a synonym for 'speed'; this is misleading since in 99% of studio work, technique has far more to do with accuracy, feel, and taste... An exercise I learned from (guitarist) Dean Parks involves setting the metronome at the slowest tempo and playing staccato quarter-notes along with it. Try it sometime—it's hard as hell."

David Hungate/Toto; Nashville Studio Bassist

CCR BAION STYLE

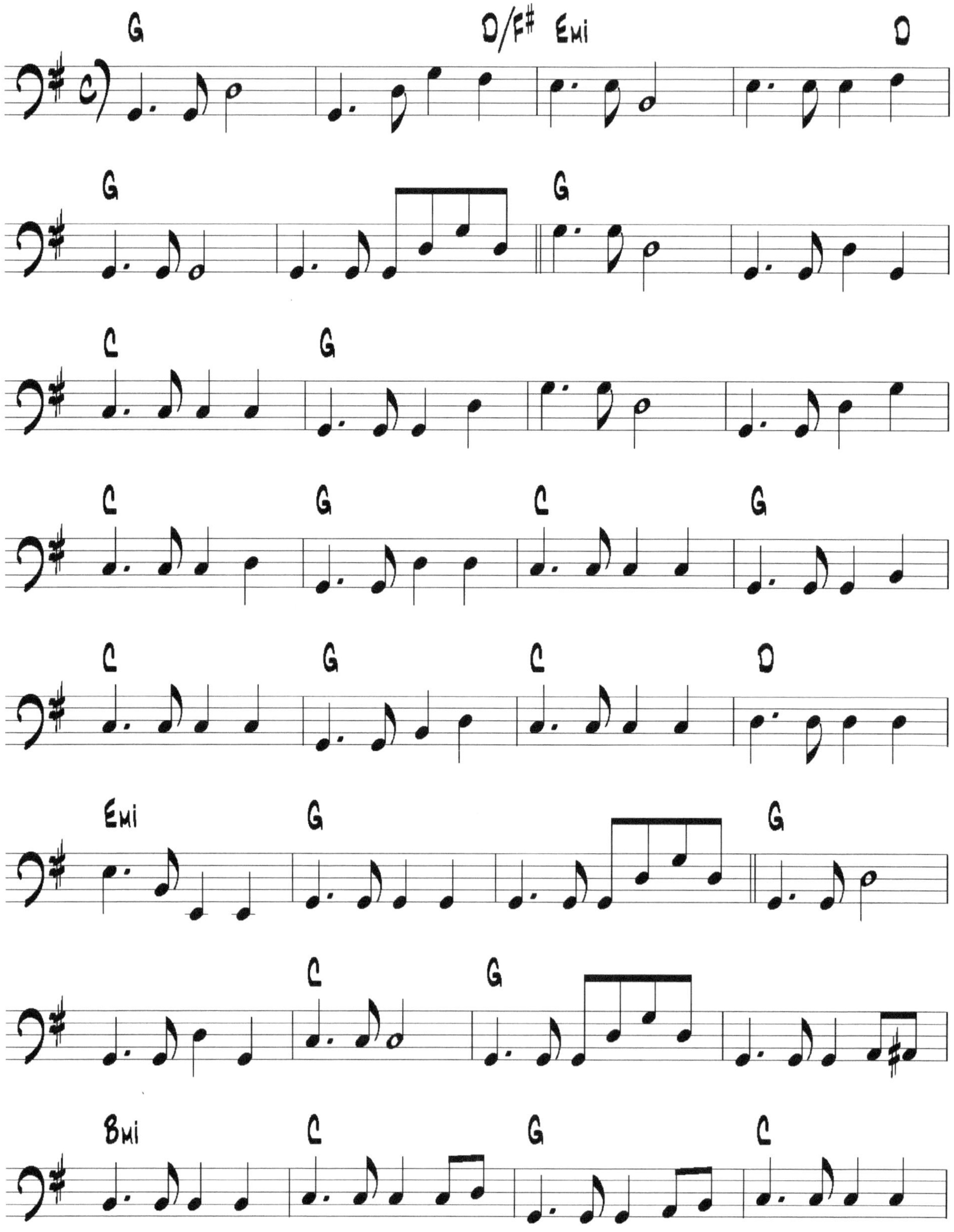

"Bass tabs are a myth. The 'lie' was started back in ancient Egypt, when the aliens landed and forced mankind to build those radio towers we call 'pyramids'. The conspiracy has grown 1000 fold, to include any form of guitar based music, including bass guitar... It's just a tool to keep our minds from discovering the truth.

You're being controlled!!!! BAWAAAAHAHAHA!!!!!!!!!"

Wes Rhoades/Bass Newsgroup

ELVIS PRESLEY BAION STYLE

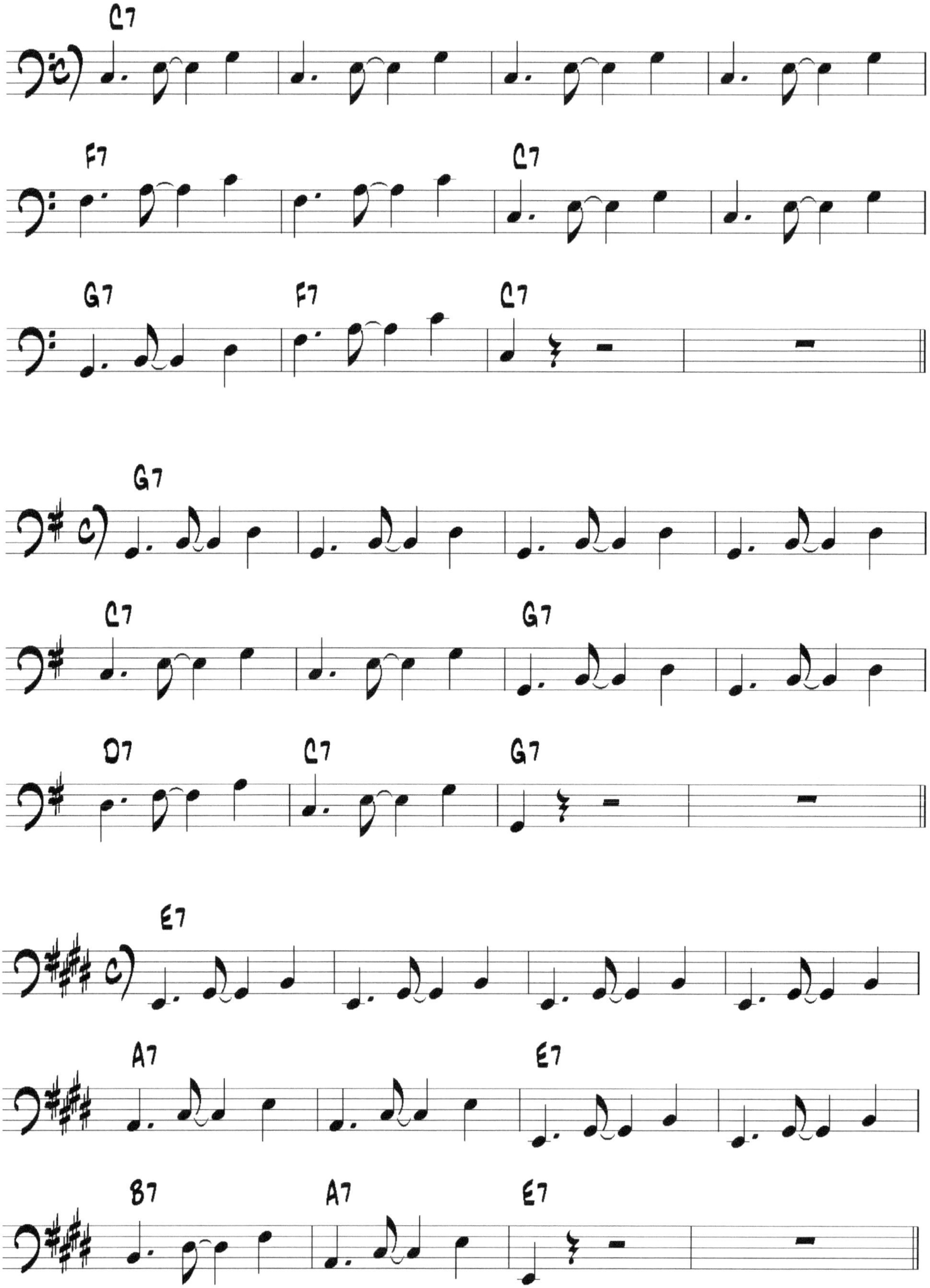

BOSSA NOVA VARIATIONS

1

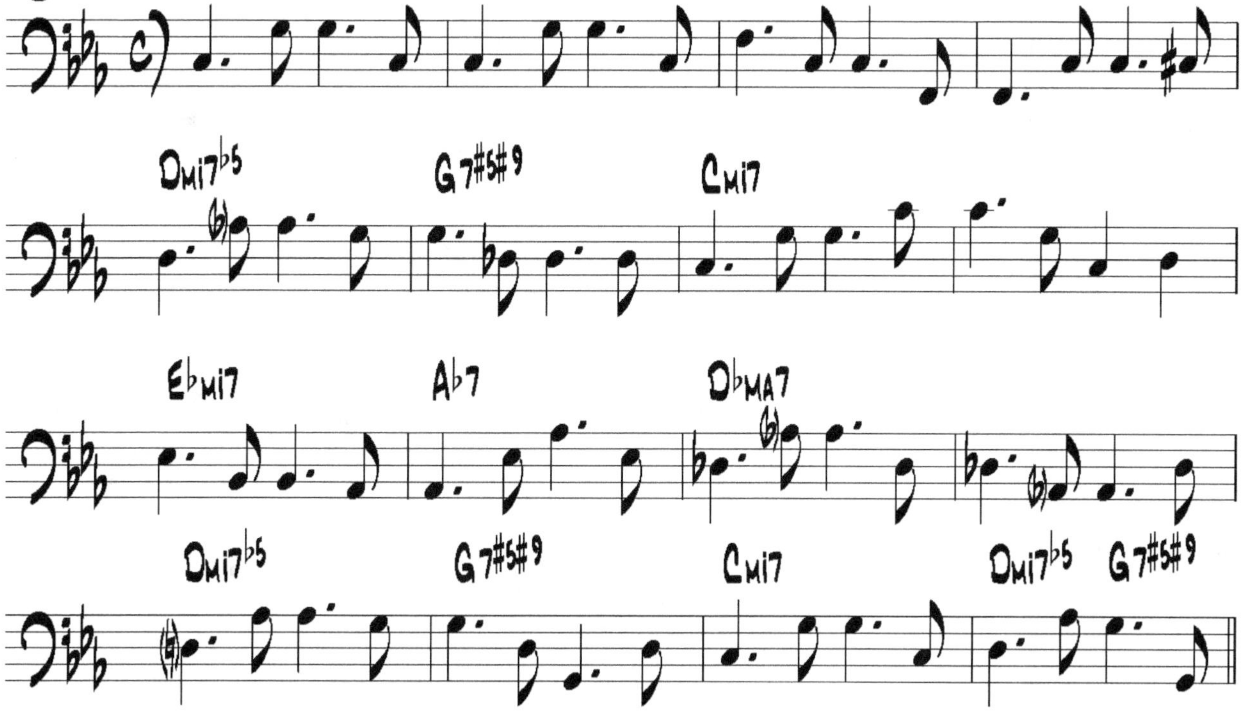

2

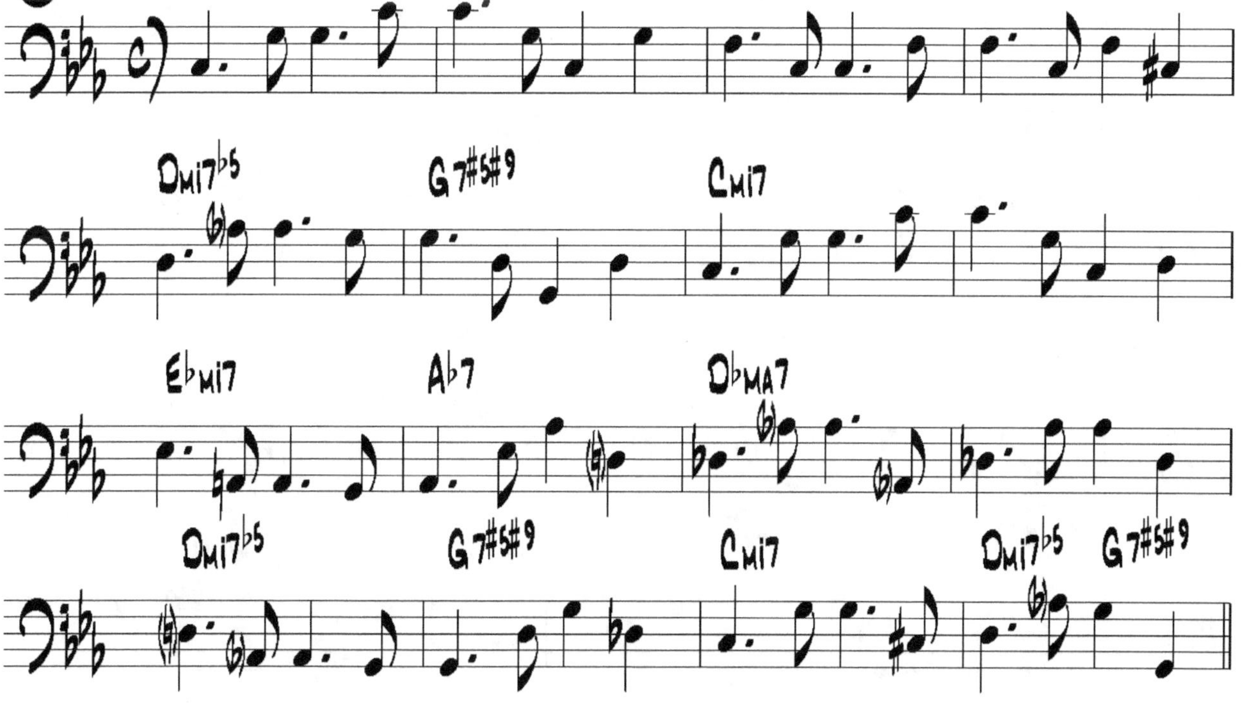

3
CMI7
FMI7
DMI7b5
G7#5#9
CMI7
EbMI7
Ab7
DbMA7
DMI7b5
G7#5#9
CMI7
DMI7b5
G7#5#9

4
CMI7
FMI7
DMI7b5
G7#5#9
CMI7
EbMI7
Ab7
DbMA7
DMI7b5
G7#5#9
CMI7
DMI7b5
G7#5#9

"You avoid the 'clinical' approach by using your ear. It is extremely important to involve your ear in process of editing your ideas."

Gary Willis/Tribal Tech

71

JOHN McVIE POCKET STYLE

Review page 36

SANTANA BAION STYLE

Review pages 50-51

73

THE SIXTEENTH NOTE

Next in line is the SIXTEENTH NOTE, which is achieved by dividing the quarter into four equal parts. COUNT: 1 e & a 2 e & a 3 e & a 4 e & ah.

"During the 30 years of my career, I've found that the best players are usually the ones who have the experience of playing many traditional rhythmic concepts. A steady diet of jazz, rock, R& B, country, Latin, funk, classical, West Indian, folk, and pop music makes for a musically healthy player."

Chuck Rainey

FREDDIE KING/"DUCK" DUNN STYLE 1

"*Remember, whenever learning something new, never think of it as being hard.*"

Victor Wooten

FREDDIE KING/"DUCK" DUNN STYLE 2

"Practicing with a metronome or drum machine is crucial! Your job description as a rhythm-section musician is rhythm... Everyone should have a metronome or drum machine when they practice."

Leland Sklar/L.A. Studio

FLEA'S 16th NOTE FINGERSTYLE

ROCCO PRESTIA'S 16th NOTE FINGERSTYLE

"The bass is the bands heartbeat. You need a blue-collar worker, dependable, steady, and relentless, to play it."

Wynton Marsalis/Trumpeter

SIXTEENTH NOTE COMBINATIONS

1

1 & 2 & 3 & 4 &

2

1 e & a 2 e & a 3 e & a 4 e & a

3

1 (e) & a 2 (e) & a 3 (e) & a 4 (e) & a

4

1 e & (a) 2 e & (a) 3 e & (a) 4 e & (a)

5

1 e (&) a 2 e (&) a 3 e (&) a 4 e (&) a

6

1 e (& a) 2 e (& a) 3 e (& a) 4 e (& a)

7

1 (e &) a 2 (e &) a 3 (e &) a 4 (e &) a

"When you leave an open space, the next note just gets bigger and bigger."

Kenny Gradney/Little Feat

78

16th NOTE RHYTHM STUDIES

 *"The bass player is the house into which all the other players come to find shelter and have a good time. If you forget that responsibility, you're leaving everybody without shelter."*

Major Holley

19

20

21

22

23

24

25

26

27

"I enjoy creating the pocket that makes the band sound good. That's my reward. I'll block for you all day long so you can run for touchdowns."

Bob Cranshaw

"Being supportive is what bass playing is all about--being there for the musicians who are playing the higher-frequency instruments. I try to do my thing, but being supportive is my goal."

Flea/The Red Hot Chili Peppers'

"I've always maintained I don't play bass, I fill space. What you leave out is just as important as what you put in. If everyone tries to fill the spaces, it muddles up everything."

Rick Danko/The Band

16th OCTAVE TECHNIQUE

SLUR NOTATION

A *hammer-on* is produced first by playing a note with the right hand, followed up a "clubbing" motion with a left hand finger to a notes of higher pitch.

To produce a pull-off, place two fingers on the notes to be sounded. Strike the first note with a right hand finger, and with picking, pull the higher left hand finger off (3rd finger, for example) to sound the second lower note (1st finger for example)

To slide from one note to the next, strike the first note and the slide the same left-hand finger up or down to the second note without releasing pressure from the sliding finger.

PHIL CHEN'S "POPPA TOP" STYLE

CLASSIC "DUCK DUNN" 16th STYLE

"I don't have great chops. What I do have is a sense of vision--being able to play two great notes rather than ten mediocre ones."

Mike Gordon/Phish

CLASSIC 16th ROCK LINES

"I never really listened to bass players. To me, it was all just sounds and feels--the Motown Sound, Memphis, Atlantic. The names came later: James Jamerson, Duck Dunn, Jerry Jemmott, Chuck Rainey."

Rocco Prestia/Tower Of Power

HEAVY METAL BALLAD STYLE

"I really want to learn from other players. Not just bassists but also horn players, singers, and electronic musicians. As long as my hands and eyes are connected, I'll keep absorbing and running whatever I've learned through my filter an keep spittin' back out."

Jason Newsted/Metallica

CLASSIC 16th NOTE R&B LINES

THE 8th NOTE TRIPLET

Divide the intro three EQUAL parts, and you arrive at the 8th note triplet rhythm.

BASIC 8th NOTE TRIPLET APPLICATION

METALLICA/RAVEL (BOLERO) STYLE

IRONSIDE RIFF: SAY AS YOU PLAY

The following "Say As You Play" will have you working up the neck one last time—many keys, many different positions.

NOTATING THE SHUFFLE RHYTHM

The shuffle rhythmic approach is based on the triplet rhythm, and it seems like there would be ONE clear cut way to notate the triplet shuffle—NOPE. There are a few different ways to notate the triplet shuffle. This FOCUS ON RHYTHM will examine the shuffle rhythm in various ways in order to get a better understanding of the shuffle.

① The *Shuffle* rhythm is based of the triplet rhythm (vocalized: doo–ee–aaah).

② The *Shuffle* feel is what you get when you emphasize the "1" and "let" portions of the rhythm: **1** trip **let 2** trip **let 3** trip **let 4** trip **let**. The most accurate way of notating a shuffle is as follows (vocalized: doo...baa....)

...but you'll rarely see it written this way...

③ Instead, you'll often see it written like this (not to be confused for the dotted 8th/16th variation associated with the 16th note rhythm)

doo ba doo ba doo ba doo ba
1 let 2 let 3 let 4 let

④ Less accurate, but more common is the directive to shuffle the 8th. In doing so, you can notate the shuffled 8th note with normal 8th notes—LESS INK = LESS CONFUSION (YEH!!)

Shuffle Feel

doo ba doo ba doo ba doo ba
1 let 2 let 3 let 4 let

ROCK SHUFFLE 1

Shuffle 8th Feel

"Most of my musical knowledge comes from playing experience."

Jaco Pastorius

ROCK SHUFFLE 2

GREEN DAY/MIKE DIRNT TRIPLET STYLE

TOMMY SHANNON/SLOW BLUES STYLE

IN THE LISTENING ROOM: SHUFFLIN'

The best way to learn capture the rhythmic nuances of "the shuffles" is simply to listen to music that... uh... shuffles.

CLASSIC ROCK

"Some Kind Of Wonderful" by Grand Funk Railroad
"Midnight Rambler" by The Rolling Stones
"Jesus Just Left Chicago" by ZZ Top
"Rainy Day, Dream Away" by Jimi Hendrix
"Still Raining, Still Dreaming" by Jimi Hendrix
"Lazy" by Deep Purple
"Boom Boom (Out Go The Lights)" by Pat Travers
"Doctor My Eyes" by Jackson Browne
"Reelin' In The Years" by Steely Dan
"Pretzel Logic" Steely Dan
"Home At Last" by Steely Dan
"Lovin' Touchin' Squeezin'" by Journey
"So This Is Love" by Van Halen
"Steamroller" by James Taylor
"Smackwater Jack" by Carole King
"Roadhouse Blues" by The Doors
"Same Old Song & Dance" by Aerosmith
"Freeway Jam" by Jeff Beck
"The Jack" by AC/DC
"Ride On" by AC/DC
"Heartache Tonight" by The Eagles
"Detroit Rock City" by KISS
"Bad To The Bone" by George Thorogood

R&B/SOUL

"Pride & Joy" by Marvin Gaye
"How Sweet It Is (To Be Loved By You)" by (Marvin Gaye)
"This Time Is Real" by Tower Of Power
"Bag's Groove" by Cornell Dupree
"Madison Time" New York Rock & Soul Review
"The Way You Do The Things You Do" by The Tempatations
"Baby Love" The Supremes
"Jimmy Mack" by The Marvelettes
"Don't Mess With Bill" by The Marvelettes
"Rockin' Chair Blues" by Ray Charles
"Isn't She Lovely" by Stevie Wonder
"Doing It To Death" by James Brown
"634-5789" by Eddie Floyd
"Livin' For The Weekend" by The O'Jays

JAZZ

"Nighttrain" by Jimmy Smith
"Fannie Mae" by Jaco Pastorius
"Don't Give It Up" by Larry Carlton
"Route 66" by Nat King Cole Trio
"Sweet Sucker" by Housten Person
"Doolin'" by Horace Silver/Sarah Vaughan
"Killer Joe" by Quincy Jones
"Blues For Mickey O" by Pat Martino

ADVANCING THE 8th TRIPLET RHYTHM

"*Learn tunes. Learn melodies. Most bass players make the mistake of just learning bass lines and nothing else. But you have to concentrate on learning a piece of music thoroughly, which includes melody and harmony and theory, as well... all bass players should become more melody-conscious.*"

Jaco Pastorius

MOTOWN TRIPLETS (JAMERSON)

www.ingramcontent.com/pod-product-compliance
Lightning Source LLC
LaVergne TN
LVHW081334060426

835513LV00014B/1281